NOT FORGETTING NORMAN
A Spitfire Pilot

Written by Stuart Palmer
Edited by Laura Jayne Palmer

Dedicated to all who paid the ultimate price during WWII
so that future generations could be free.

To truth and to honour.

In memory of Barry Pellow.

PROLOGUE

Dear readers, the story you are about to follow is true. It is based on actual events as researched by the author and is dedicated to all the brave aircrew who gave their lives in the name of freedom during World War 2. The story revolves around the circumstances that caused the death of two Spitfire pilots in the skies over Cornwall during March 1942. It also goes on to describe how the author, through his own research, discovered that nothing is ever as it seems. A story that appears to be cut and dry hides a long lost secret.

Sergeant William David Norman was a young Australian airman, who came to England to fly Spitfires for the RAF. Unfortunately during March 1942 he was killed in an accident whilst flying his Spitfire, serial number AB496. Now instead of that being the end of the story, for me it was just the beginning.

Sgt Norman would have had no idea that his death would be the start of an incredible, long and personal journey seventy-five years later. By telling his story I hope to ensure that his name will be spoken again and not just lost in time together with his sacrifice and that of countless others.

There is another aim in telling Sgt Norman's story. That is to right a wrong that was instigated in the immediate aftermath of this tragic accident, and repeated again seventy-five years later. However, this can only happen if the authorities take notice.

I ask you, the reader, to follow in my footsteps and to understand that this story was never about blame. It is about the truth. The airmen referred to in this story were incredibly brave, of superb character and doing an impossible job in often-impossible circumstances. They were all heroes and the truth will never detract from that.

Certain people within certain organisations referred to within these pages will no doubt have their feathers ruffled (they will know who they are). I make no apologies for that, as they had their chance to put it right, but chose not to.

The accident that killed Sgt Norman was a collision with another Spitfire. Whilst I am not going to dwell too much on the service records and histories of both pilots prior to this event, I feel it is pertinent for us to get to know Sgt Norman, because he is the focus of this story. I will introduce you to the other pilot later, who also sadly lost his life in the accident.

CHAPTER 1
Sergeant William David Norman

Sgt William David Norman was born on the 20th September 1916 in Melbourne to an English father, William David Norman (Senior), and Australian mother, Alice Mabel Norman. Sgt Norman enlisted on the 16th August 1940, number 404315, as an aircraftsman 2nd class at nearly 24 years old. He trained in the CAC Wirraway (Fig 1.) and on the 7th April 1941 he was promoted to Sergeant.

He embarked at Sydney on the 27th May 1941 bound for Britain, leaving behind his parents and sister, Iva Mabel (Smith, 2000). He disembarked at Belfast and on the 30th August 1941 he joined No 3 Personnel Reception Centre (PRC). On the 5th September 1941 he joined No 57 Operational Training Unit (57 OTU) and finally on the 21st October 1941 he was assigned to No 66 Squadron, who at the time were based at RAF Perranporth in Cornwall. The squadron moved to RAF Portreath (Fig 2.) during December 1941.

The squadron, under the command of Squadron Leader B. L. Duckenfield AFC was waiting to be equipped with the new Spitfire VCs (Fig 3.), which started to arrive on the 1st March 1942. These Spitfires carried two cannons, four machine guns, and a jettisonable fuel tank. The arrival of the new Spitfires saw the promotion of Sqn Ldr Duckenfield, and on the 3rd March 1942 the new commanding officer arrived – Sqn Ldr Daniel E. Cremin DFC. Sadly Sqn Ldr Cremin was to be the other pilot involved in the mid air collision that would occur later that month.

CHAPTER 2
The Collision

On the night of the collision Sgt Norman was flying Spitfire AB496, which was one of the seventy Vs delivered between February and September 1942 (Halley, 1985). It was first flown on the 17th January 1942, and was powered by a Rolls Royce Merlin 45 engine (World Naval Ships, 2001a). Sqn Ldr Cremin was flying AB462, which was part of the same batch of seventy Vs. His Spitfire was built at Supermarine (dispersal) and first flew on the 14th February 1942 (World Naval Ships, 2001b). It was powered by a Rolls Royce Merlin 46 engine (Fig 4.).

During the beginning of March prior to the accident it was noted that on the 14th March 1942 Sqn Ldr Cremin tried out the new jettisonable fuel tank, dropping it on to the airfield from 300 feet. On the 20th March 1942 Sgt Norman and Belgian pilot Sgt Hoornaert were in the air on an interception patrol, but nothing was spotted.

The 24th March 1942 saw RAF Portreath carrying out its routine duties. Later in the day Sgt Norman and Sqn Ldr Cremin practiced dusk landings, and at 2120 hours on a clear moonlit night the pair were wheels up for night flying practice. They would never see wheels down, because at 2205 hours they collided in mid air south of St Erth, killing both pilots. The last radio transmission and the statement of a local Home Guard witness, who heard a crash and saw one plane spinning in, afforded the conclusion that they were formatting and hit in mid air.

The 30th March 1942 saw the coffin of Sqn Ldr Cremin put onto a train bound for his home town for a private funeral with Flight Lieutenant Friendship and Pilot Officer Darby as escorts. In the afternoon the squadron attended the funeral of Sgt Norman at St Illogan Church.

A report dated the 27th March 1942 within Sgt Norman's records (NAA, 2020) states that Sgt Norman "was coming into formation on Sqn Ldr Cremin and just ran into him... It is thought that the accident was due to Sqn Ldr Cremin permitting one so inexperienced in night flying to fly in formation on him without more careful briefing."

A summary of the incident (Storr, 2006):
"Spitfires AB496 flown by Sgt Norman, and AB462 frown by Sqn Ldr Cremin (RAF) took off from RAF Station Portreath Cornwall, detailed to carry out night flying practice. The weather was clear with moonlight. During the practice the aircraft collided in the air. AB462 spun in minus its starboard wing and AB496 dived vertically into the ground. No chutes were used and both pilots were killed. AB496 crashed at Frythens Farm in St Erth, Cornwall. A subsequent Court of Inquiry into the accident found that AB496 had misjudged the distance between itself and AB462, and it collided with the starboard side of the fuselage and main plane of AB462."

The police log entries (Supt. Rowland, 1942) for the incident are as follows:
"25.03.42 – Supt. Rowland reports that at 2155 hours on 24.03.42 a British Spitfire aircraft crashed in field on Trevessa Farm (fig 5.) 1¼ miles southwest St Erth Police House (Camborne Division). Machine badly smashed and burnt out. One occupant dead. Machine from RAF Stn Portreath no AB496"

"25.03.42 – Supt. Rowland reports that at 2155 hours on 24.03.42 a British Spitfire aircraft crashed in field at Frythen Farm (fig 5.) 1½ miles southwest St Erth Police House (Camborne Division). Machine badly smashed and burnt out. One occupant dead. Machine from RAF Stn Portreath no W.AE651." (Please note that the serial number of this aircraft is completely wrong. AE651 was actually a Hudson that was damaged by fire at Setif on 2nd December 1943).

I suspect there is good reason why the serial number of AB496 was readily noted and that of AB462 was mistaken. I am going to mention Supt. Rowland's (1942) next entry as well, because this incident does figure in my story:
"25.03.42 – Supt. Rowland. 1522 hours 25.03.42 at Rosevidney Farm, Ludgvan 1½ miles northeast Crowlas Police Station a British Hampden Bomber, no unknown, crashed - completely burnt out. Crew four safe."

A further entry confirms the serial number as AT118. The Spitfire spinning in minus its starboard wing is also verified by a police log entry dated the 12th April 1942 made by Supt. Rowland (1942) which states: "A farmer found a machine gun and ammunition in a ploughed field at Trevessa Farm St Erth 1 mile south St Erth Police House which had evidently fallen from a British plane." I will follow up on this entry later. Also please note that there was no inquest into Sqn Ldr Cremin's death at this stage.

At this point I ask the reader to pause momentarily, just to be sure that you have completely understood the circumstances of the collision as documented. This historical documentation becomes more important as we progress. It will also, I hope, help you to realise and understand the frustration and sometimes anger I felt towards certain organisations that are included later in the story. They are completely blinkered and fail to grasp what actually happened here. They refuse to acknowledge they must be wrong and, as a result, arrive at all the wrong conclusions.

You might want to grab a cup of tea at this point, as we fast-forward seventy-four years to 2016...

CHAPTER 3
Initial Enquiries

I always had a massive interest in World War 2 aircraft ever since I was a young boy, and so came the time when I decided to start researching World War 2 aviation in Cornwall as a hobby. I became intrigued by aircraft that had crashed. I thought it would be a good idea to produce a map of every crash site I could identify and combine that with as much detail about each incident as I could find, including any eyewitness accounts. Eventually I planned to write up my findings in one comprehensive document.

I knew time was not on my side, as we are quickly losing a generation of people who could recall these events happening. I also was not prepared to accept hearsay about a crash site. It was of great importance to me that I physically located evidence of a crash site with a metal detector as absolute proof.

On a point of legality, when I started this exciting new journey I was completely unaware of The 1986 Protection of Military Remains Act. I merely thought I could discover some small remnants of aircraft that would support my research and as long as I had the landowner or farmer's permission that was all I needed.

Two incidents initially caught my attention, mainly because they happened close to where I live in Hayle, Cornwall. The first incident was the Spitfire collision at St Erth, and the second was a Handley Page Hampden (AT118) at Rosevidney. These two incidents happened within a day of each other and potentially also within a mile of each other as reported in the crash log (Knight, 2007) at the time.

Mid-July 2016 saw me seeking permissions to search the farmland I was interested in, and I would like to take this opportunity to thank Andrew Badcock and family of Trevessa Farm and Frythens Farm, Andrew Davey of St Aubyn Estates, Roger Richards of Trevabyn Farm, Sir John Nott of Trewinnard Manor, and finally Garnet and Edna Hocking and their family of Tregethas Farm. Having introduced myself and explained what I wanted to do, all the landowners were happy and enthusiastic about my project, and permissions were granted on the basis that I respect the land, which went without saying.

Andrew Badcock of Trevessa Farm told me that somebody had located a crash site and recovered aircraft remnants a few years earlier, and led me to the spot. He did not know anything about the second site. He also showed me the barn at Frythens Farm (Fig 6, fig 7.) where the bodies of the two pilots were allegedly stored overnight. Naturally I needed to confirm this site for myself and I was eager to try out my brand new Garrett ATX metal detector, which I had bought especially to do this job, as I did not want to risk missing that crucial fragment of aircraft.

CHAPTER 4
The Search

Later I conducted a search of the area that Andrew had pointed out to me at the top of the field near the boundary. Sure enough I found some remnants just below the surface, which was a pleasant surprise considering this site had already been heavily detected. I also found remnants spread out some distance away in a northerly direction. This site was now a confirmed crash site (fig 8.).

At this point I was unable to confirm whether this was the resting place of Sqn Ldr Cremin's AB462 or Sgt Norman's AB496, so for the time being this site will be referred to as the 'higher southerly site'. There was an assumption made by previous researchers that this site belonged to AB462, because there was no deep penetration, and it fitted the description of Sqn Ldr Cremin's aircraft spinning in. At the time I also latched onto this assumption, as I had no reason to doubt it, and the remnants and debris I found supported the idea of a spin in rather than a vertical dive. The search was now on for Sgt Norman's AB496 which in theory could be anywhere on Trevessa Farm, as the site was long ago lost in time and memory.

To be honest, at this point I was more interested in the Hampden AT118 at Rosevidney, so I went to see the owners of Tregethas Farm, as I believed their land was a good place to start. It was at this point that I met Garnet Hocking and his mum, Edna, whose help and enthusiasm has been invaluable.

Edna had been interviewed previously and repeated to me that she recalled the night she heard the collision of two aircraft over Frythens Farm, and that the police were out with torches looking for body parts. Garnet was able to point to the field at Frythens Farm where he believed one Spitfire had crashed, and he was right. It was the higher southerly site. The field was clearly visible from Tregethas Farm, as the land sloped upwards. He was unaware of the location of the second crash site. Garnet and Edna went on to tell me about the Lancaster that came down on a boundary wall of the high fields to the rear of their farm the following day. I explained that it was actually Handley Page Hampden AT118 that had crashed, but that it had the same dual-fin configuration (Fig 9.) as the more well-known Lancaster (Fig 10.) and misidentification was easy to forgive. In fact the only Lancaster crash in Cornwall occurred on 17th December 1942 at Errisey Farm, Grade Ruan. The serial number was W4359 and all the crew were sadly lost. I eventually located the crash site of AT118 (Fig 11, fig 12.) on 18th December 2016 having split my time between the two search areas.

During this time I had built up a good relationship with Garnet Hocking, and he knew of a man that had spoken about the two Spitfires. The man had been fourteen at the time of the crash, and lived in St Erth. Garnet said he would go and speak to him on my behalf and ask if we could meet. The man's name was Barry Pellow.

Garnet arranged for us both to go and see Barry for a chat at his house in St Erth. His son David and daughter Mary were present, as Barry was quite fragile and his hearing was poor. It was a pleasure talking to Barry and listening to his recollections. His son and daughter said later that it had made Barry really happy to be able to reminisce about the old days, and it was all he could talk about. Crucially for me, Barry's account of the events of the 24th March 1942 would prove to be accurate and invaluable.

Barry recalled, "I was fourteen at the time when two Spitfires came low and fast over St Erth late one evening. There followed loud bangs. The lads from the village ran to see the crash. The plane on the hill was up near the hedge with its nose looking upwards. The lower plane dived into the ground with smoke and fire coming from the pit where it had buried itself. A wing came off in Trevessa Farm just behind the farmhouse. The local boys dug some of the bullets from the wing and took them home. Later the police came looking for the lads and they had a good telling off."

I showed Barry a Google Earth image of the area and once he had got his bearings he was able to mark where the two Spitfires had hit the ground. The one on the hill was exactly where I had found the relics. The lower site was just through a gateway off the track to Frythens Farm. I showed him where the gateway was, as I had been through it, and he said, "Yes, just through the gateway." This confused me a bit, as I had already detected this area. I told Barry I had already searched the field with my metal detector and he replied, "You won't find it with no metal detector boy, it's far too deep and they filled the hole over." I also kept thinking about the police log that named the second site as Trevessa Farm, not Frythens Farm.

CHAPTER 5
Finding Spitfire AB496

I spent some time going back over the field Barry had spoken about as well as land at Trewinnard Manor and Trevessa Farm, but Barry's account of the events kept niggling at me. He was so sure. So, on the 1st May 2017 I returned to Frythens Farm and the field with the gateway. It was only then that I realised the field between Frythens Farmhouse and the one I had been searching also had a gateway off the track just a stone's throw away. This goes to show how easily you can be thrown off-course by relying on recorded documentation that turns out to be far from accurate.

I entered the field and could not believe it when more or less my first signal twenty to forty feet into the field uncovered a piece of twisted aluminium, followed by more relics. I was absolutely elated. I had finally found AB496 after the site had been lost for seventy-five years (Fig 8).

This discovery meant so much to me. Following all my research and fieldwork we had two known pilots' graves and now I finally had two known crash sites. It was the final piece of the puzzle. Or so I thought. I made a point of going back to see Barry to tell him I had found it and how, even after all these years, he was more or less spot on. He was over the moon and kept saying, "Told you boy, just through the gateway."

Barry's son and daughter, David and Mary, had dug out some local wartime newspaper cuttings that Barry had kept concerning other local incidents. They also showed me something very special. It was a tiny moulded model aeroplane, which had been made by Barry's wife's father, Mr Murley. It was stuck to a piece of card that had written on it, "My father made this from a piece of the canopy of a Spitfire which crashed into a field on Frythens Farm in Long Lanes during the war." I thought this was poignant, so took photographs of the model (Fig 13.) and newspaper cuttings (fig 14.).

I last spoke with Barry on the 23rd January 2019. Just over two weeks later on the 9th February 2019, Barry Pellow passed away.

CHAPTER 6
A Disturbing Discovery

Back on site at Frythens Farm after working the area, it became clear that there was a definite central concentration of deeper metal detector signals, and the more I enlarged the dig the stronger the signals became. I would like to think that I was quite meticulous with the process of removing the finds. I took my time to ensure I recovered every fragment carefully. After all, I had found a piece of history and I was pursuing my dream. I took photographs, logged dates, cleaned and carefully stored. The range of finds was staggering and I cherished every one of them. I think this work ethic and care of the job in hand ensured the survival of what I found next.

Andrew Badcock had been brilliant in supporting my efforts looking for AB496. When I told him I had found it he erected a perimeter around the site to protect it from livestock. Nothing was too much trouble for him, and it meant I would not have to backfill the hole when I vacated at the end of the day.

On my return I was carefully tracing a mangled piece of pipe (Fig 15.) that just kept going deeper. As I removed the soil I exposed something I never expected to find... bone! It appeared to be a joint, like a ball and socket. I immediately stopped digging, as the bone appeared to go deeper into the ground. I contacted Andrew who immediately came down to the site. We discussed the possibility of it being an animal bone, as we were aware that the bodies of both pilots had been recovered and had known graves. It felt like too much of a coincidence that we were stood on an aircraft crash site looking at what we both thought were the remains of a human lower limb. It was an easy decision to shut the site down, protect it, and call the police.

From this point on the story gets embroiled in officialdom, as you would expect. Please stick with me as I walk you through it to the end. Remember that what you are reading in minutes, actually unfolded over months and years for me, which means you get to the twist in the story much sooner than I did.

I met with the police and subsequently a member of the Cornwall Archaeological Unit (CAU), who confirmed the remains to be human. The coroner and the Ministry of Defence (MOD) were duly informed of the discovery. I was contacted by the MOD Police Investigation Team, who explained that in order to excavate a military crash site a licence is required, but that I was not in any trouble, as they accepted that I had not knowingly done anything wrong. I was simply pursuing a hobby.

I remained keen to be involved with the pending process and was advised to give my contact details to the CAU so that I could be present during the excavation. As I understood it, the procedure would be that the coroner would advise the Joint Casualty and Compassionate Centre (JCCC) to issue a licence to the CAU in order for them to recover the human remains for identification. The remains of the aircraft were secondary. Once the JCCC were happy that all the remains had been recovered I could then apply for a licence to recover what still remained of the aircraft in the ground, including the Merlin 46 engine, assuming this had not been recovered by the CAU.

Remember that as far as I was concerned I had located the crash site of Sgt Norman's Spitfire AB496. This was the aircraft that had struck Sqn Ldr Cremin and had then dived vertically into the ground, with Sqn Ldr Cremin's Spitfire spinning into the ground minus its starboard wing. The site that I located and the subject of the CAU excavation will be known as the 'lower northerly site', and that is how Barry recalled it, "The lower plane", "With smoke and fire coming from the pit."

I patiently waited for the call from the CAU regarding a date for excavation. It was only through my own curiosity that I called Andrew Badcock to see if he had heard anything. He told me, "Yeah Stu, that happened weeks ago. Didn't you know?" No I did not know.

I was also in regular contact with the JCCC while they waited for the CAU's report and the results of the DNA testing on the recovered remains. Once this had been achieved the family would be informed and the remains interned at the original grave. I thought what a great outcome that would be, and I looked forward to it very much. Sgt Norman could finally rest in peace and not lie in some forgotten field. Fair enough, the circumstances were not ideal, but the outcome would be.

When I next spoke to the JCCC they informed me that cross-referencing the DNA with that of a surviving family member had now identified the remains, and the remains 100% belonged to Sqn Ldr Cremin. My reply was, "You mean Sgt Norman?"

"No, Cremin," she replied.

"Right okay," I said, and hung up the phone quite puzzled. Obviously DNA does not lie, but this result left me with more questions than answers. I had also asked about the licence application, but was told to wait as the JCCC had not yet received the CAU's full and final report.

You can only imagine my thoughts. According to all the historical documentation, this was Sgt Norman's crash site, with a vertical impact, and located at the lower northerly site as identified by Barry Pellow. There could only be two possible explanations: The first explanation is that Sqn Ldr Cremin was flying AB496 that night, which is highly unlikely and I believe can be discounted. The alternative is that Sqn Ldr Cremin flying AB462 struck Sgt Norman, who was flying AB496, causing AB496 to lose its starboard wing and spin into the ground, with AB462 diving vertically into the ground. In other words, the complete opposite of the historical documentation! How and why could this massive error in the reporting of the incident have happened, even at Sgt Norman's inquest?

CHAPTER 7
A Lot of Confusion

Was this a simple documentation error or was the incident documented this way deliberately? I do not believe it was an error by the police, as all the evidence was right in front of them on the ground, with serial numbers, recovered remains, a wing missing from one crash site, and many other factors. All the evidence, I believe, points to a deliberate cover up of the actual events.

The reason I believe this is that Sqn Ldr Cremin was an experienced and highly decorated pilot, as well as the Commanding Officer of 66 squadron at the time. Sgt Norman was a trainee and, in the big picture, a nobody. I believe it sat more comfortably with the authorities at the time to make the accident Sgt Norman's fault.

I stated at the beginning of this story that it is not about blame, it is simply about the truth, and one thing I did know for sure was that the truth lay in that back-filled crater in a remote field in Cornwall. Obviously I thought the CAU would have all the answers in their report, having carried out the excavation, and I looked forward to having access to the report and being able to recover the remains of the Merlin 46, but once again I had to be patient and wait.

I heard nothing from the CAU, so I contacted the JCCC again. They had received the CAU's full and final report and, based on their findings, I was verbally informed there and then that there would be no chance of a new licence being issued to excavate the site further as the CAU had indicated that there may still be human remains present. It was now a classified war grave and the sole aim of the JCCC was the protection of the remains. I have absolute respect for the JCCC and fully understand their position, as they can only act on the information they are given, regardless of how puzzling that information is. However there is an aspect of the reasoning behind the decision that I want to address later in this story, and it will be highly controversial.

I never wanted to end up in a situation of myself versus the CAU, but this is now unavoidable. However I do not want to lose sight of my motivation. This is a story foremost about Sgt Norman, and making sure his name is spoken again. The nature of his sacrifice must not be forgotten, and the record of the incident needs to stand corrected. I am a firm atheist, but I believe we have an energy; a spark that does not die with the flesh. Now imagine two incredibly brave Spitfire pilots on a loop, taking off from Portreath on night flying practice every year on the 24th March and fatally colliding at 2205 hours, their energy never moving on. All because somebody chose to lie about what happened.

Here lies the issue: the truth can now never be proven, as the CAU did not complete the job they were commissioned to do by the coroner. They should have recovered all human remains from the site, and they should also have recovered the Merlin 46. However the CAU's lavish 49-page report (Sharpe, 2017) states that they have removed all human remains from the crater, because they excavated down to undisturbed subsoil and they have declared the crater sterile. An email from the CAU (Young, 2018) stated that, "It was not in our remit to excavate the whole field." However in their report they state that all remains would be telescoped and contained within the crater on the vertically impacted crash site that is now sterile. But this is not a vertical impact is it? It is Sqn Ldr Cremin's crash site, a spin in. Oh, and there was no Merlin 46 recovered. It seems confusing, but I believe I have made sense of it and can walk you through it.

The bottom line is that, thanks to the CAU repeating the mistakes and arriving at the same incorrect conclusions that were made in March 1942, our two Spitfire pilots are still not at peace and I am now on a mission to help them. The CAU's lavish report is quite informative in some areas as it gives a lot of background information, but unfortunately as far as the memory of Sgt Norman is concerned, and the conclusions drawn, I believe it is a massive fail.

The way I see the situation is that we have Sqn Ldr Cremin's DNA at the lower northerly site, so if the Merlin 46 I believe is still in the ground has been recovered, it would confirm that the aircraft was AB462 and the damage to the propeller would tell us whether it struck AB496 or if it was still rotating when it impacted the ground.

CHAPTER 8
The Report

For a moment I considered stopping this story, as it was starting to seem like the one thing I was trying to avoid, a witch-hunt against the CAU, rather than a memorial to Sgt Norman and indeed Sqn Ldr Cremin. I do not understand why the CAU did not listen to me, and work with me to achieve the right outcome. Unfortunately it is now impossible to tell the story without exposing the failings and shortcomings of the CAU.

The CAU report (Sharpe, 2017) contains many contradictions, for example "The aircraft hit the ground whilst travelling from the south west." This is not possible, as both aircraft were seen and heard flying over St Erth seconds before the collision and subsequent impact with the ground. If the direction of travel given by the CAU was correct, the attitudes of both aircraft post-impact as described by Barry Pellow would not be possible. The starboard wing would have to have been severed post-impact, and travelled a ¼ mile. Not possible. The actual direction of travel was from the north over St Erth. The location of the starboard wing confirms the flight path and aircraft attitudes post-impact. This mistake alone ensures the correct conclusion would never be achieved.

The report also states that the CAU excavation of the southern site took place on the 27th July 2017. However, it was not the southern site, but the northern site. Within the conclusions/discussion section of the report the CAU again confirm the same incorrect information that was written in 1942. Sharpe (2017) states that "The heavy engine would have become deeply buried as a result of a vertical impact," which is correct, but he then goes on to say that this site does not fit that type of impact, so concludes that the site is consistent with Sqn Ldr Cremin's shallow angle spin in, as reported in the police log. Here is the issue in a nutshell, because the DNA from the site belongs to Sqn Ldr Cremin, the CAU have had to make the site match the historical documentation.

The CAU will not accept that the evidence screams out the fact that Sqn Ldr Cremin struck Sgt Norman. The entire incident would make perfect sense if the

CAU just swapped the names around and accepted that they were excavating a near-vertical impact crash site. The report (Sharpe, 2017) also states that, "About ten years earlier a local metal detectorist identified the crash site of Sqn Ldr Cremin's plane and uncovered human remains." I only identified the crash site two months before they excavated it, not ten years! Sharpe (2017) also states that, "What happened to the other plane is not known. This plane dived into the ground." It is known! Sgt Norman was struck by Sqn Ldr Cremin, causing Sgt Norman to spin into the ground minus his starboard wing – notice I have now swapped the names to make the information correct. The higher southerly site was investigated by another detectorist years earlier and was map-referenced by him, which the farmer confirmed to me as he was shown relics. The site was also described to me by an eye witness, Barry Pellow, as being the location of the higher Spitfire which crashed with its nose pointing up to the hedgerow. This site was further confirmed by me, with a handful of finds.

The CAU also reference the Lancaster bomber that crash-landed nearby the day after the Spitfire collision. It was not a Lancaster that crash-landed, it was Handley Page Hampden AT118. To not check basic details like this is a schoolboy error. This questionable referencing occurs throughout their report. There is one instance in particular that I am going to scrutinize, because the CAU rely on it as part of their conclusion and in doing so they convert folklore to fact.

The CAU picked out a quote from Edna Hocking of Tregethas Farm who was interviewed in 2005 about her wartime experiences. The CAU labeled and filed this interview as part of their pool of well-documented information surrounding the incident. I actually interviewed Edna and I do not doubt that her recollection is based on events as she remembered them, but I will explain why I have an issue with the CAU quoting Edna's memories.

Within Sharpe's (2017) report he says that Edna recalled on the night of the collision, "The police were out in the fields looking for body parts." When the CAU submitted their report to the JCCC they advised that due to the nature of Sqn Ldr Cremin's impact (spinning in), although the crash crater was now archaeologically sterile, human remains might still be present in the surrounding field. This statement obviously meant that there could be no further excavation of this site without a licence, which would never be granted, as the site status was now a war grave.

I fully understand that when an aircraft spins into the ground at a shallow angle there would be every reason to expect a large area of debris and human remains, but the site they excavated was not a spin in! It was a near-vertical dive in and they state that a nose-diving aircraft would become telescoped and buried within a relatively small crater, which is exactly the situation at the excavated site. They found no debris field or relics outside of the crater, which does not fit with a spin in.

Based on what the CAU thought they had excavated, they produced diagrammatic mock-ups of how they imagined the crash site would have looked immediately after the ground impact. Guess what? It is all completely wrong! They have drawn the engine sat at ground level having become detached, with the bulkhead and cockpit in a partial crater (Fig 16, fig 17, fig 18, fig 19.). Because they did not find the engine, in their minds this must be what happened, but they did not find the engine because it is buried deep down. Despite this they still stated that they had dug down to undisturbed subsoil and declared the site sterile.

Interestingly the diagrammatic mock-ups would have fitted with Sgt Norman's crash site, but it was just too late for the CAU. The blinkers were well and truly on. I will draw a line under the shortcomings of the CAU for the moment. I do not believe they had the right experience to carry out this type of excavation, but I accept they probably are very good at excavating small bits of pottery and the like out of the ground.

You would be forgiven for thinking that this must now be the end of the story. After all, where can it go from here? I do not give up easily, so I will continue this story by explaining what I absolutely believe to have happened, and as a consequence what I believe still remains in the ground.

CHAPTER 9
A Different Version

The two aircraft were wheels up at 2120 hours from RAF Portreath. Immediately prior to the collision they were flying south-south-west, Sqn Ldr Cremin flying AB462 came in on Sgt Norman flying AB496 from Sgt Norman's starboard side, flying low and fast over St Erth. At 2205 hours Sqn Ldr Cremin (not Sgt Norman) misjudged his speed and distance, striking Sgt Norman's aircraft at his starboard fuselage and mainplane causing AB496 to lose its starboard wing, which fell into a hedgerow just to the rear of Trevessa Farmhouse. AB496, probably still under power, spun into the ground at a relatively shallow angle affording Sgt Norman no time to vacate the aircraft. There is a chance that Sgt Norman was severely injured or killed in the air at the moment of collision due to where the propeller of AB462 struck AB496. Either way he was killed on impact with the ground. The remains of AB496 were witnessed by Barry Pellow to be mostly at ground level in the higher field, with its nose visibly pointing up to the hedgerow. The ground conditions at this site are very rocky.

There could be an initial counter-argument that Sgt Norman came into Sqn Ldr Cremin from Cremin's port side, but when analysed and combined with what we know, this scenario becomes impossible. After striking AB496 Sqn Ldr Cremin's aircraft would have immediately lost propulsion and peeled off slightly to the west of AB496's crash line (Fig 20). It started to invert, hitting the ground at an almost vertical angle, affording Sqn Ldr Cremin no time to vacate the aircraft. The remains of AB462 were witnessed to be deeply buried in a pit of smoke and fire in a lower field adjacent to the higher field in which AB496 crashed. The ground conditions at the lower northerly site are a trough of soft soil that has been eroded down over the years. It should be noted that Barry Pellow only relayed information regarding the aircrafts' final positions, condition and locations. He did not provide any information on the planes' serial numbers. I have been able to add this information through the course of my research.

With all this information in mind, we know the bodies were recovered and we have two known graves, but we also now know that not all the remains were initially recovered from the lower northerly site. I would guess that was due to the nature and depth of impact. We must also bear in mind that in the present day incidents like this would be horrific and fully investigated, leaving no stone unturned. But back during the early years of the war these incidents were every day occurrences and the recovery teams had become hardened to their task and were not that thorough. It is no surprise then that they would have reached a point with this deeply buried Spitfire that they would probably have said, "OK that's it, we've done all we can do here," and just backfilled the crater regardless of what may or may not have remained. We must also remember that it was important to get the land working as soon as possible to feed the nation.

* * *

Before I continue, I must raise a point that concerns me. The DNA recovered from the lower northerly site is Sqn Ldr Cremin's, and his remains were interred at his known grave. The aircraft that dived vertically into the ground has always been documented as Sgt Norman's AB496, rather than Sqn Ldr Cremin's AB462. My concern is that the remains buried in 1942 could feasibly have been buried the wrong way around. So whilst the headstone at St Illogan Church says Sgt Norman is buried there, the remains could actually be those of Sqn Ldr Cremin, and vice versa. If my account turns out to be correct then surely this alone is reason to investigate further? The remains may have been buried correctly, but we just cannot be sure.

* * *

I absolutely believed the CAU would be recovering a Merlin 46 engine from the lower northerly site. The crash recovery team back in 1942 would not have recovered a deeply buried Merlin 46 from underneath the compressed remains of the cockpit containing some body parts, but left the body parts in situ. I am sure the Merlin 46 engine is still buried in the lower field, along with the serial number and damaged propeller, in other words, the key to what happened. Now all I have to do is prove it!

CHAPTER 10
A Frustrating Month

Knowing the lower northerly site could no longer be physically tampered with, I wondered if some form of non-intrusive ground survey could give me the answers I needed. My thoughts turned to geophysics, so I made some enquiries with numerous local businesses that carried out ground works. I was informed that a geophysics study could deliver the answers I was looking for especially as, despite it being smashed and degraded, I was looking for a large metal object. The downside was that it would be an expensive process, and as I am self-funded it was obvious that I would not be able to afford it.

Not one to remain downhearted for long I made some more calls and was eventually advised to contact Cornwall School of Mines. I spoke with Neill Wood, the Programme Director of Surveying and Land/Environmental Management. I explained what I wanted to do and why. Neill was extremely interested in my story, but confirmed that the process I was requesting was very expensive. However I had given him an idea about how we might be able to achieve my request, and I was to leave it with him for a few days and he would be in touch.

A couple of days later I received a call from Neill. He asked me if I would like to have the survey done for free! He explained that he had a mature student who was looking for a suitable subject for his dissertation towards his Master of Science by Advanced Study in Surveying and Land/Environmental Management, and that my World War Two crash site would be perfect. It would obviously become the student's project, but I could have full access to the data. As you can imagine I was over the moon! This was great news and I could not wait for the process to start.

With the kind permission of Andrew Badcock of Trevessa Farm I met with Neill and his student, Spencer Julian Allin known as Julian, at the crash site. We exchanged all the relevant information and they were both as excited as I was, after all for them this was a unique opportunity to survey a below-surface crash site, which was virtually unheard of. The data provided combined with my research could provide invaluable referencing for future geophysics examinations. To emphasise how much achieving this milestone meant to me I am going to spell it out in full:

Neill Wood, Programme Director of Surveying and Land/Environmental Management at Camborne School of Mines, College of Engineering, Mathematics and Physical Sciences would be supervising Julian in his dissertation towards his Master of Science by Advanced Study in Surveying and Land/Environmental Management!!

The survey took place during July 2018 with myself and my wife, Laura Palmer present. Not much was given away on the day, as the data had to be fully analysed and verified, which would take months. However on a number of occasions Julian (Fig 21, fig 22.) would look up and say, "There's something here." That was enough for me and I felt that my dedication would finally be rewarded and my justification for this book would unearth the truth that had remained lost and buried for seventy-five years. I just had to wait for the results.

*   *   *

July 2018 also saw the inquest take place into Sqn Ldr Cremin's death, as no inquest had been carried out at the time. The inquest took place on the 16th July 2018 at County Hall, Truro, Cornwall and was heard by Assistant Coroner Barrie van den Berg. Sqn Ldr Cremin's death was recorded as being due to multiple injuries and was classed as an accident (Van den Berg, 2018). Nobody will ever dispute this conclusion, however section three of the Coroner's report contains a concerning response to the question of the "circumstances by which the deceased came by his or her death." The response was that,

"On the 24th March 1942 Daniel Cremin was killed in a midair collision after his Spitfire was struck by another pilot resulting in fatal destruction of both aircraft," (Van den Berg, 2018)

The coroner could only come to this conclusion based on the information he had in front of him: the report from the CAU, which I believe is flawed. Reading the coroner's report makes my blood boil for Sgt Norman. Seventy-five years later and with all the available resources the experts have access to they should have at least noticed that something did not quite add up.

When I questioned the CAU about whether they knew what they were doing, I received an email response (Young, 2018) that basically suggested I should not question them. I replied to them explaining that while I do not have letters after my name, I am absolutely sure I am right about what happened on the 24th March 1942. I accepted that this still makes me a nobody in their eyes, but that the whole story is about a nobody. Except that that nobody is Sgt William David Norman who travelled from Australia to fly Spitfires for the RAF. He perished doing that job and I vowed to make sure his name is spoken again.

*   *   *

By publishing this story I am ultimately trying to force a reaction from someone: the JCCC, the CAU and the Air Historical Branch (AHB). Why? Because when I presented them with my new evidence and research they did not challenge me or even respond.

CHAPTER 11
The Truth

The months passed as I waited for Julian to complete his dissertation, which I received during January 2019. It was a brilliant piece of work, but as you can imagine very technical and full of words and diagrams that were beyond my understanding. I understood words like "anomalies" and "debris field", which made the report (Allin, 2018) sound very encouraging.

I emailed Neill Wood and asked him if he could give me the data in layman's terms, basically was there a Merlin 46 engine still in the ground? In his reply Neill directed me to some of the diagrams in Julian's data (Fig 23, Fig 24, Fig 25, Fig 26, Fig 27) and said that, whilst he is not an air crash investigator, the data shows an "intense magnetic anomaly on the right is suggestive of an engine," (Wood, 2019) but that it is out of the main debris field and quite deep. Wood (2019) states that the data indicates "disturbed ground to the full depth of the survey. I would interpret this as the fingerprint of the engine having buried itself. My best guess would be that it is more than four metres (thirteen feet) deep, perhaps quite a bit more."

Neill's reply was music to my ears. At last I finally had confirmation that the lengths I had gone to were totally justified. Also the brilliant witness account from Barry Pellow proved to be true and accurate. I went on to properly read and digest Julian's dissertation and was able to grasp more about what the data and images meant combined with Julian's summaries.

The data described the CAU's excavation pit as a featureless void. However the debris fields can be seen exiting the pit and are obviously wing imprints. Interestingly within these two debris fields there are anomalies, which Julian Allin (2018) surmises could be remains of armament or undercarriage, and of course the large anomaly we believe to be the Merlin 46 engine. The CAU's report includes pictorial mockups of how they believe the aircraft impacted with the ground and the scene immediately after impact. The new data completely rubbishes this interpretation just as I was sure it would.

Armed with this exciting new evidence I was keen to submit it to the JCCC, believing they would be keen to reinvestigate and allow further excavation of the site, under licence, to obtain the truth. Bearing in mind the CAU had declared the impact crater sterile, the retrieval of the engine is crucial in confirming AB462's identity along with Sqn Ldr Cremin's DNA, and the propeller would hold the secret to which aircraft caused the collision. The record could finally be rewritten and the two pilots could rest in peace. So I sent a lengthy email containing all the new evidence and research to the JCCC asking them to consider permitting a new licence to re-excavate the site, as obviously there were many questions that demanded to be answered. I also copied the CAU and AHB into the email.

The JCCC replied on the 27th March 2019, standing their ground and stating that no further licences could be issued and no further excavations of the site could take place because of the possibility of human remains being present. They said the results of the geophysics survey should be placed in the Cornwall Historic Environment Record, as it is an archaeological site. Also within this email something strange was written, "Once the serial number of the aircraft you uncovered was confirmed as Spitfire AB462." My issue is that the aircraft's identity has never been physically confirmed by myself or by the CAU. The aircraft has been assumed to be AB462 because of the DNA match to Sqn Ldr Cremin. The only way to confirm it 100% would be to excavate the rest of the aircraft along with the Merlin 46 engine, which it seems nobody wants to happen.

Interestingly I had no response whatsoever from the CAU or AHB. No challenge, no defense, nothing! Silence speaks volumes.

CHAPTER 12
A Visit to Sgt Norman

On the 1st December 2019 I did something that for some reason I had never done before: I visited St Illogan Church (fig 28.) to locate Sgt Norman's grave. I found it amongst 52 war graves at the churchyard and, despite my beliefs in the afterlife, I knelt by his grave and found myself talking to him. He died at 2205 hours on the 24th March 1942, and I had stood on that spot. He was buried on the 30th March 1942 and now I was stood on that spot. I know so much about him it felt so personal. I told him that I knew what had happened that night, but that I too was alone with nobody listening. I promised to see this through to the end and that I will never give up. I stayed for a while and was momentarily joined at his grave by a robin.

At the bottom of Sgt Norman's headstone (fig 29.) it reads, "Tell England he died for her and here he lies content."

That inscription brought a tear to my eye, as it is so lovely. But if only he knew how England has betrayed his memory. All anybody wants is the truth. Nobody is judging the participants of this tragic event, but I am frowning upon those who have written, and continue to support, flawed records about the event.

CHAPTER 13
An Unfinished Story

I am hoping my words will prompt some kind of reaction from those who can make a difference to the records. It is obvious to all of you what I think should be done. It is now my goal to get Sgt Norman's story into the public domain and read by as many people as possible. I realise there is no guarantee my thoughts will ever be read by others, which would no doubt suit certain previously-mentioned organisations. However as far as Sgt William David Norman is concerned, somebody spoke his name again and cared enough to put pen to paper in order to tell the truth.

Here is the controversial bit. I mentioned earlier that I have an issue with the term "war grave", in particular with how the term is applied in this situation. The CAU made it quite clear to me that it would have been better if this site had not been disturbed in the first place, but would it? Here is my opinion on it. I am only going to talk about World War Two aviation crash sites, and only a limited number that fall within the category that is up for debate.

The whereabouts of many sites including mine are not actually known other than general information about which farmland the site is on, but there are two known graves for the deceased pilots from the crash I was researching. As far as I am concerned, the site I found was not a known war grave until I made it so by placing it on a map and discovering human remains. Now, the powers that be would say that because of the fact both pilot were killed and the nature of the impacts, there could be human remains still present and in this case there were.

I now understand The Protection of Military Remains Act (1986) and I understand that something had needed to be done as prior to the introduction of the Act the world and his wife were digging up everything in a completely irresponsible fashion, not logging and recording finds, and as a consequence much has been lost. There were also recovery teams who did great work and were acknowledged. Post-1986 in order to excavate a military aviation crash site a licence has to be issued by the JCCC after specific criteria has been met. It appears that if the crash was a fatal one a licence would automatically be refused even if there are known graves, with the reason being that human remains may be present. Ordnance may also be an issue, but not an automatic refusal.

Now I am aware of this initially you might think it is an obvious refusal, because nobody wants human remains to be dug up. But I do not think it is as simple as that. I will use my site as an example, because I am not talking about underwater wrecks or inaccessible sites. My site turned out to be a normal flat field used for grazing livestock with absolutely no access issues. If I had been aware of the procedure at the time of finding my first fragment of Spitfire and applied for a licence it would have been refused, as it was a fatal crash. Even when the CAU were supposed to have recovered the remains and declared the site sterile, a licence to excavate was still refused due to the site being classed as a war grave.

I'm sorry, but this is just unacceptable. It is not a war grave and it is not desecrated ground. It is a field in the middle of nowhere. There is no dignity in that. These sites should be identified and fully excavated like any other archaeological site. My site was given the opportunity but the effort failed massively. I suppose the label "war grave" costs nothing. No action required.

For some the notion of aircrews' remains being buried with the remains of their aircraft in an unknown field at an unknown location might have an air of romance to it, and surviving descendants may wish to leave it this way, but I believe they should be given a choice. A team should be set up to physically identify as many sites as possible with a pin on a map. Surviving descendants could then decide whether or not to excavate and, if not, at least they would have the exact location.

Another consequence of this "leave it unknown and call it a war grave" mindset is that the farmers and landowners could quite innocently carry out drainage or ground works on a site without even knowing, completely destroying it. Where is the romance in that? Imagine descendants and relatives of the deceased aircrew visiting the crash site for a moment of reflection and to pay their respects, but wondering if that piece of bone they noticed in a badger set or drainage ditch could actually be part of the remains of their deceased relative. This may sound blunt, but under the present mindset this scenario is entirely possible.

I think it is clear where I stand on this matter, but I suspect it is more about cost and resources. Bear in mind that as the years pass so do the eyewitness accounts, the information passed down through generations, and ultimately the physical remains in the ground. The sites will become totally lost in time and with them the Normans and Cremins.

There is one final point to end this debate. In more recent times when loved ones have gone missing presumed dead, and with no remains to be found, if information came forward about the whereabouts of the location of a body, would we leave it there? No, I don't think so. So what is the difference?

It is all about one thing. The truth. Knowing the truth and finally laying it to rest.

"You are not forgotten"
Sgt William David Norman
Sqn Ldr Daniel Edward Cremin DFC

Fig 1

Fig 2

106G/UK 166 3 12 JULY 46 F/20" 1541 SQDN.
3051

Fig 3.

© IWM CH 5429

Fig 4.

Fig 5.

ST ERTH VILLAGE

TREVESSA FARM

FRYTHENS FARM

(50°09'20"N 5°25'59"W) 3 km

Fig 6.

Fig 7.

Fig 8.

ST ERTH VILLAGE

AB496 STARBOARD WING & MACHINE GUN
AB462 CRASH SITE
AB496 CRASH SITE

TREVESSA FARM

FRYTHENS FARM

(50°09'20"N 5°25'59"W) 3 km

Fig 9.

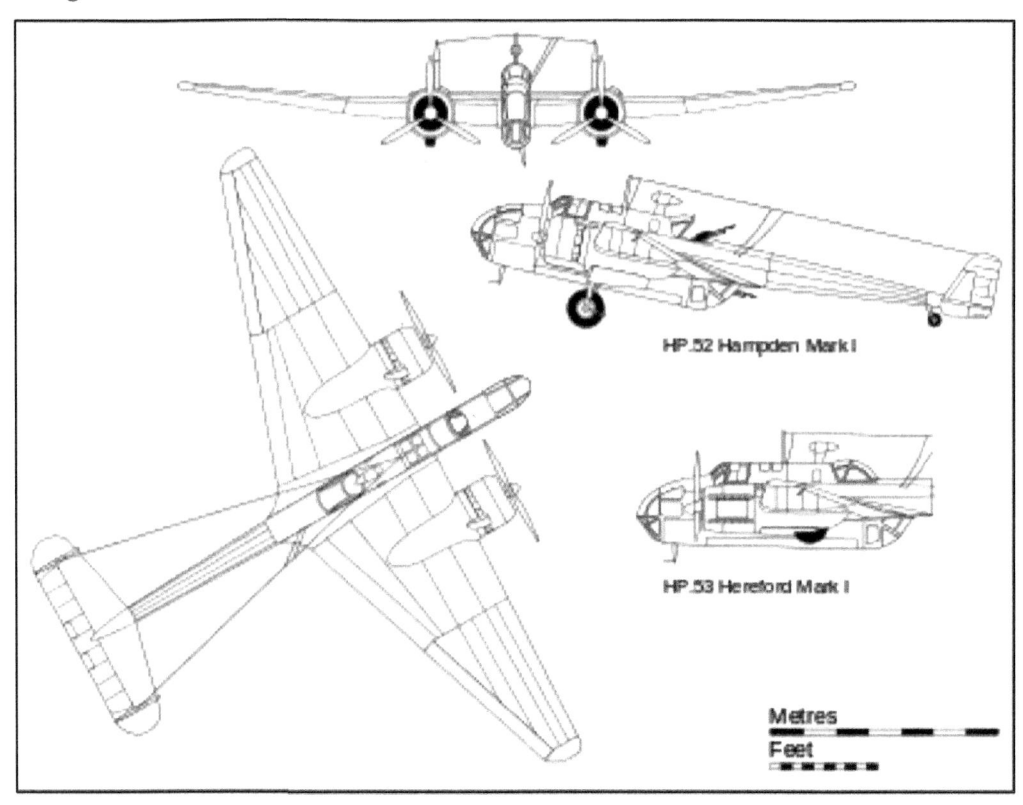

HP.52 Hampden Mark I

HP.53 Hereford Mark I

Fig 10.

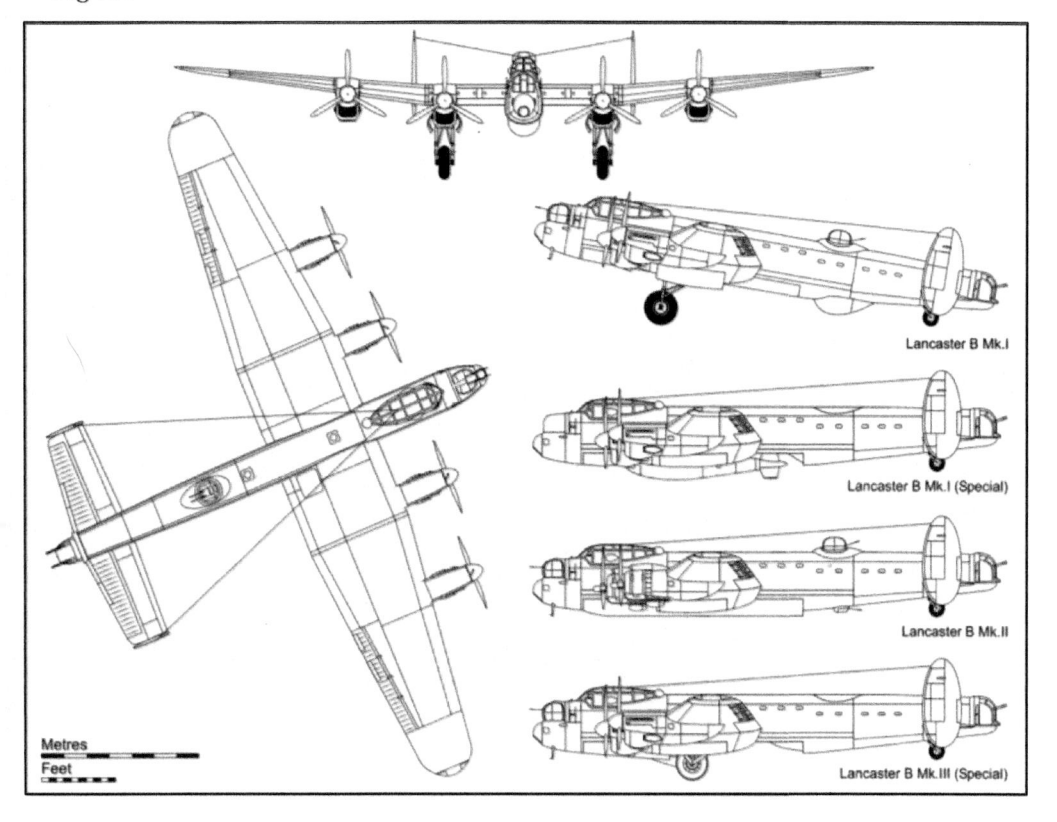

Lancaster B Mk.I
Lancaster B Mk.I (Special)
Lancaster B Mk.II
Lancaster B Mk.III (Special)

Metres
Feet

Fig 11.

Fig 12.

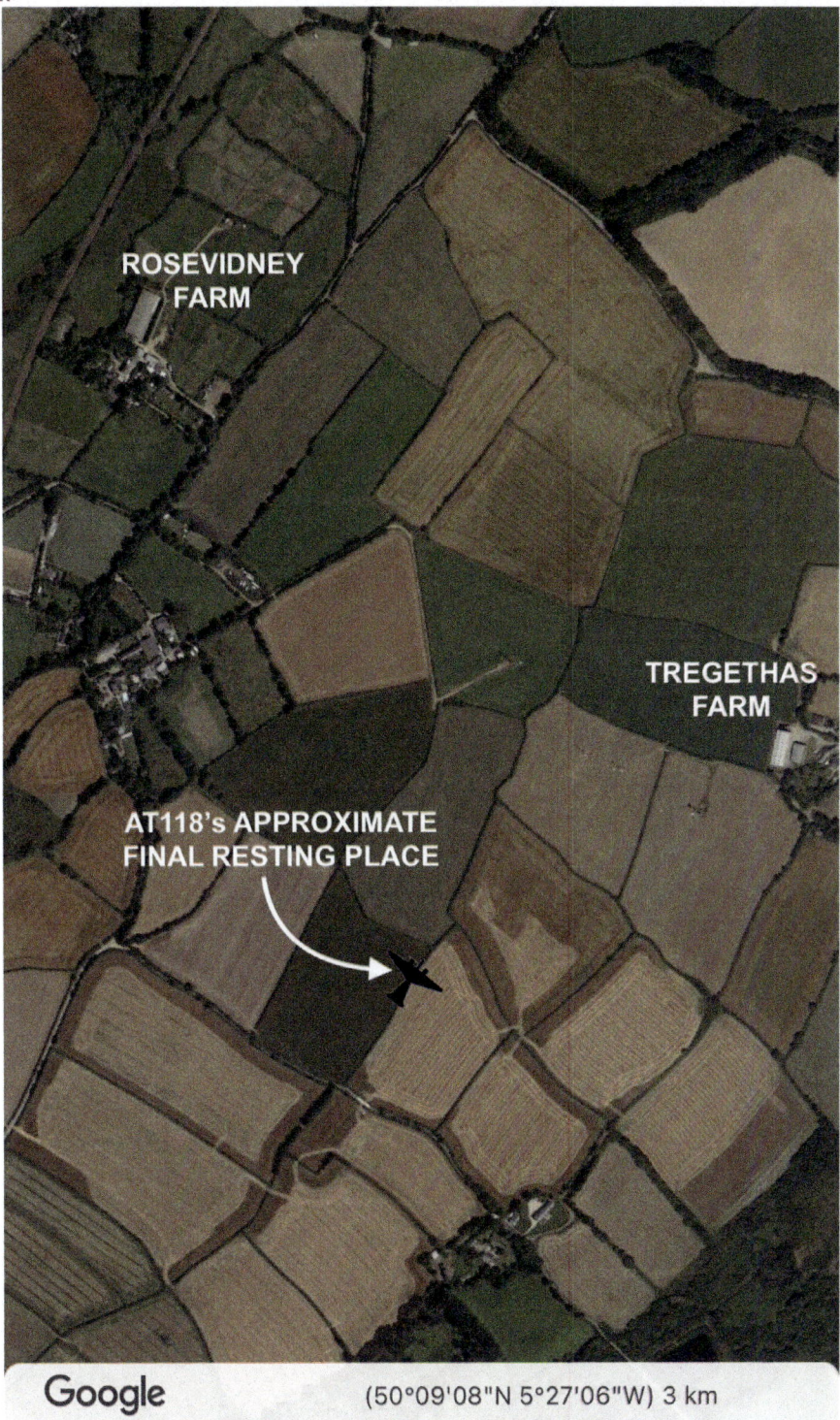

ROSEVIDNEY FARM

TREGETHAS FARM

AT118's APPROXIMATE FINAL RESTING PLACE

(50°09'08"N 5°27'06"W) 3 km

Fig 13.

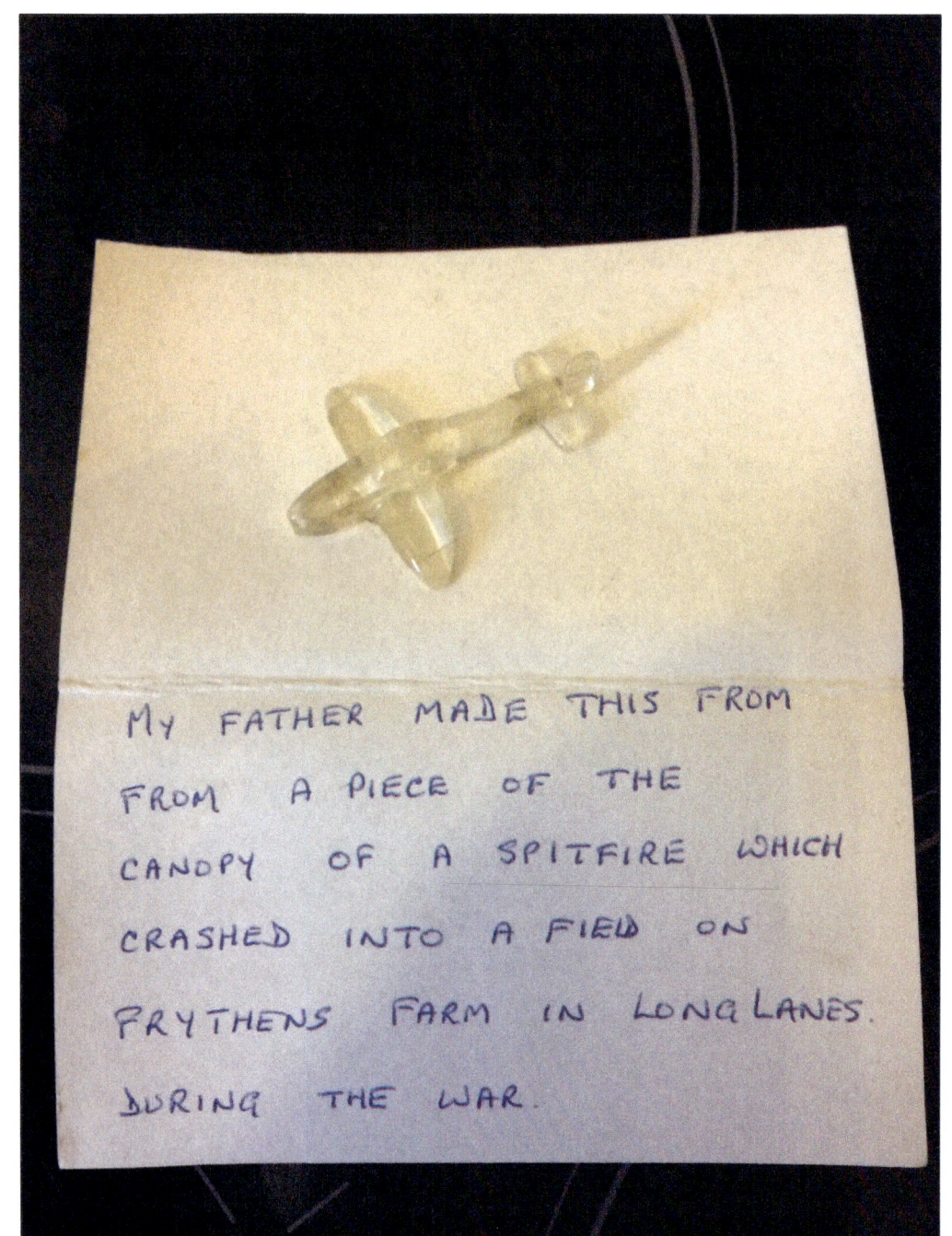

MY FATHER MADE THIS FROM FROM A PIECE OF THE CANOPY OF A SPITFIRE WHICH CRASHED INTO A FIELD ON PRYTHENS FARM IN LONG LANES. DURING THE WAR.

Fig 14.

Fig 15.

Fig 16.

Fig 45. Crash stage 1. The Spitfire hits the ground at an angle of 30^0, its wings shear off and the body begins to telescope into the rear of the engine block.

Fig 17.

Fig 46. Crash stage 2. Engine block shears off at firewall; the remainder of fuselage impacts the rear of the engine block and the fuselage burial angle changes to 60°. The cockpit area begins to crush and fragment.

Fig 18.

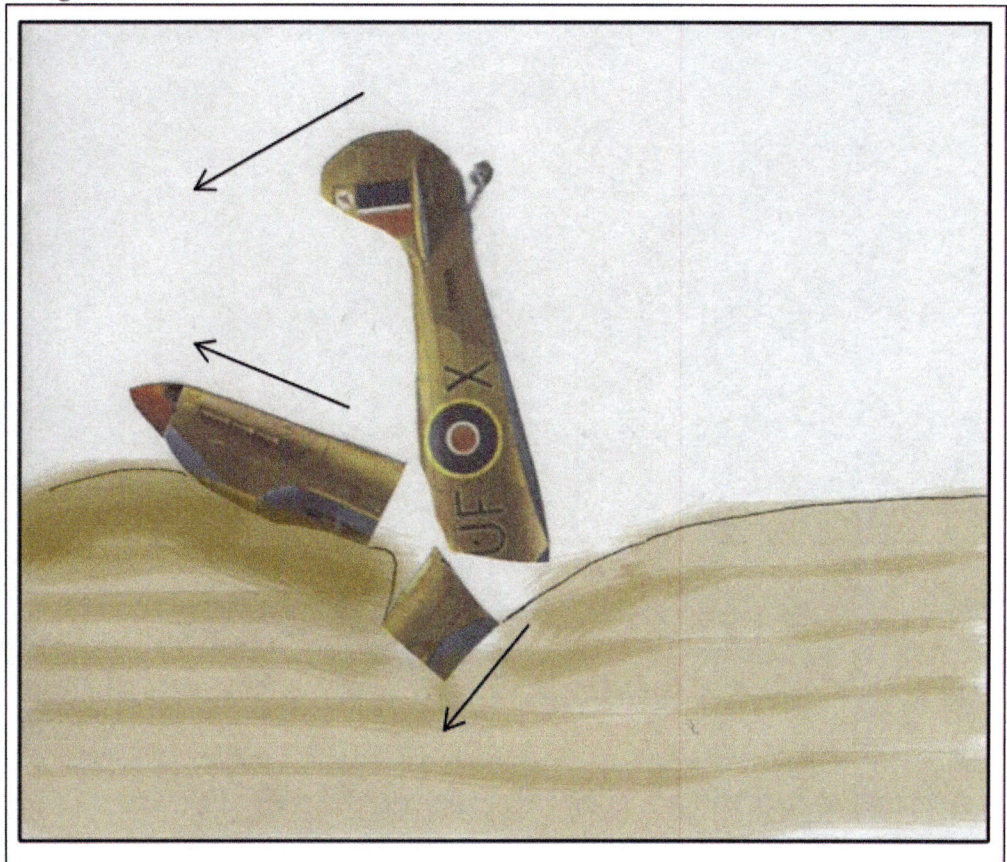

Fig 47. Crash stage 3. The engine block continues to move away from the crater; the crushed remains of the centre part of the cockpit is buried in the crater; the mid fuselage and tailplane shears off and is carried forwards in the direction of impact.

Fig 19.

Fig 48. Crash stage 4. The engine block comes to rest (probably further on than shown here); the mid and tail section of fuselage may have ended up ahead of the impact crater as shown here, or standing more or less vertically on top of the crater as shown above; the fragmented remains of the mid cockpit area become buried at the base of the crater. Some above-ground parts of the aircraft wreckage are affected by fire. Above ground wreckage subsequently salvaged by the RAF maintenance unit team. The crater is partly backfilled.

Fig 20.

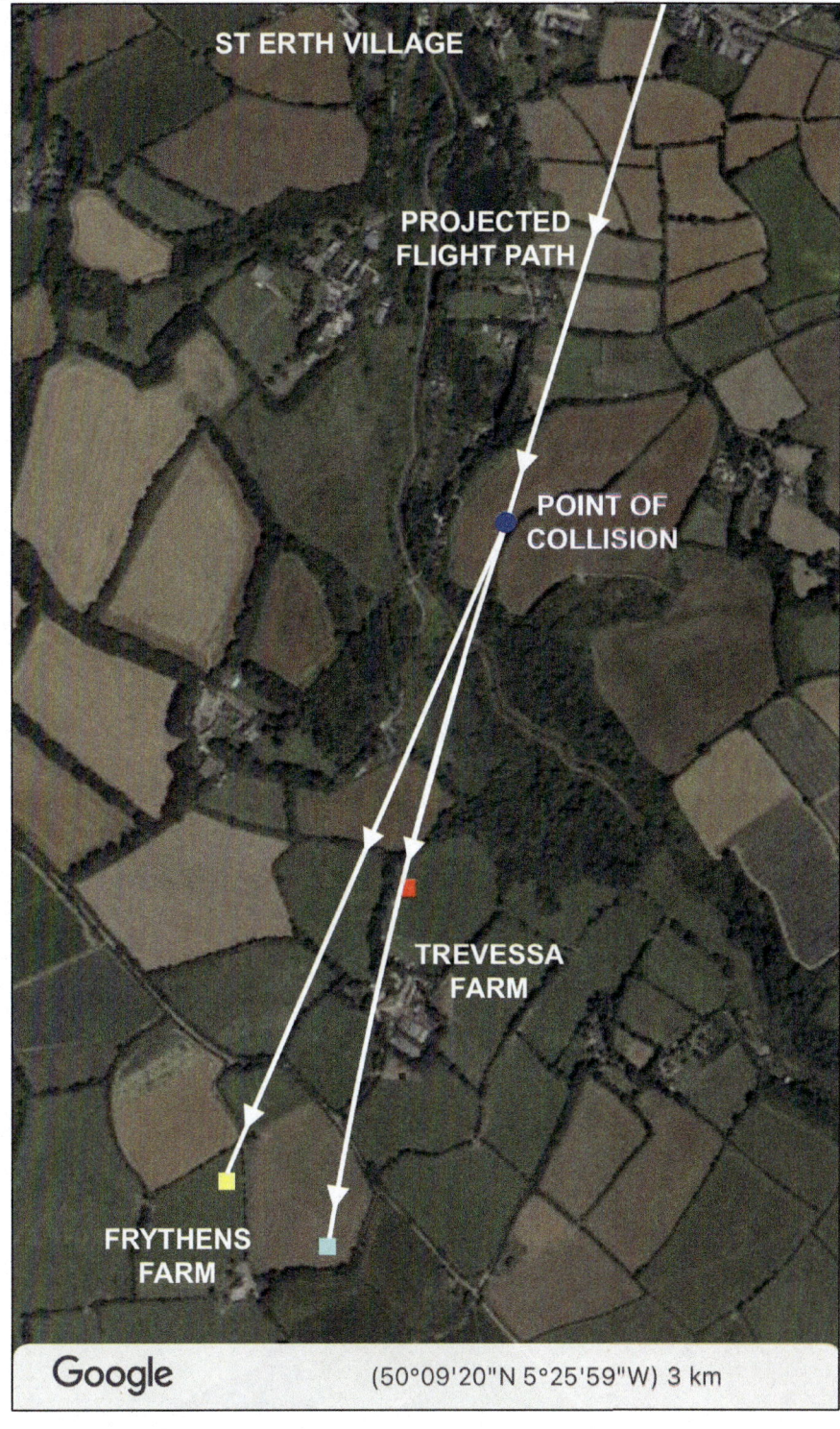

Fig 21.

Fig 22.

Fig 23.

660058953.   CSM M118 Surveying, Land and Environmental Management.

4.1 Magnetic Gradiometry Data

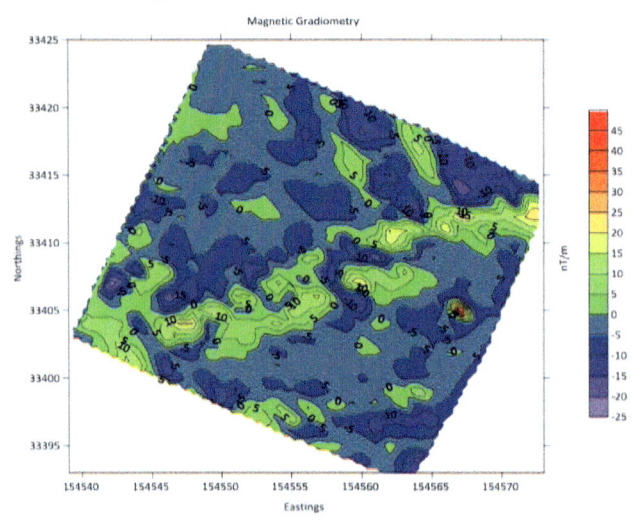

Figure 23. Magnetic gradiometry of the study grid.

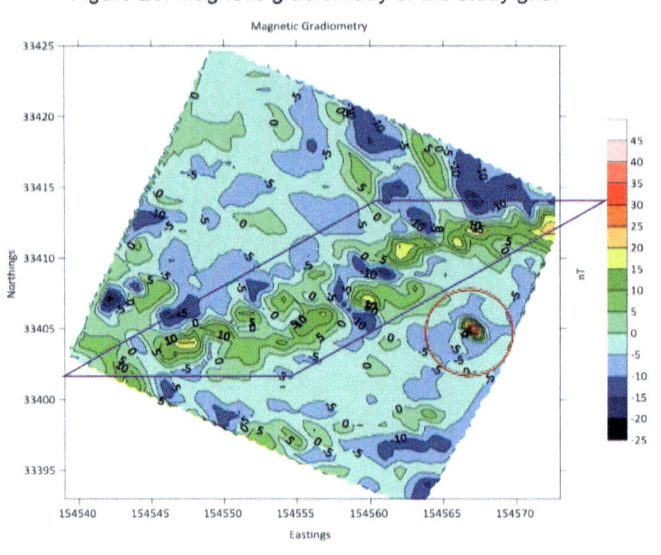

Figure 24. Magnetic gradiometry image (copy of the above) of the study grid utilising a different colour pallet to improve the contrast showing the suggested anomalies. The red circle highlights an anomaly of up to approximately 45nT,

34

Fig 24.

660058953.   CSM M118 Surveying, Land and Environmental Management.

4.3 Overlaying of the data sets

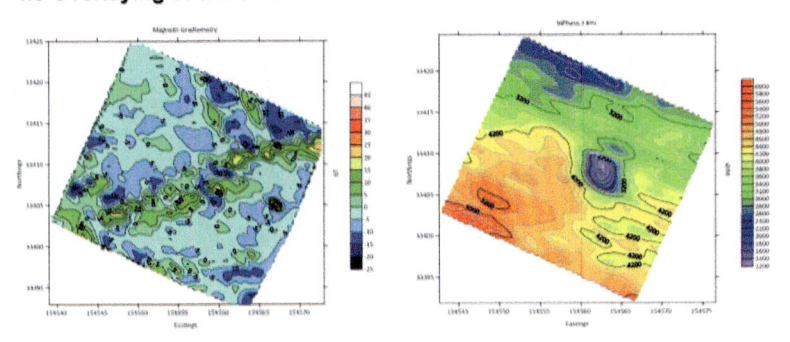

Figure 24. Mag Data from above   Figure 35. 3kHz In Phase Data from above

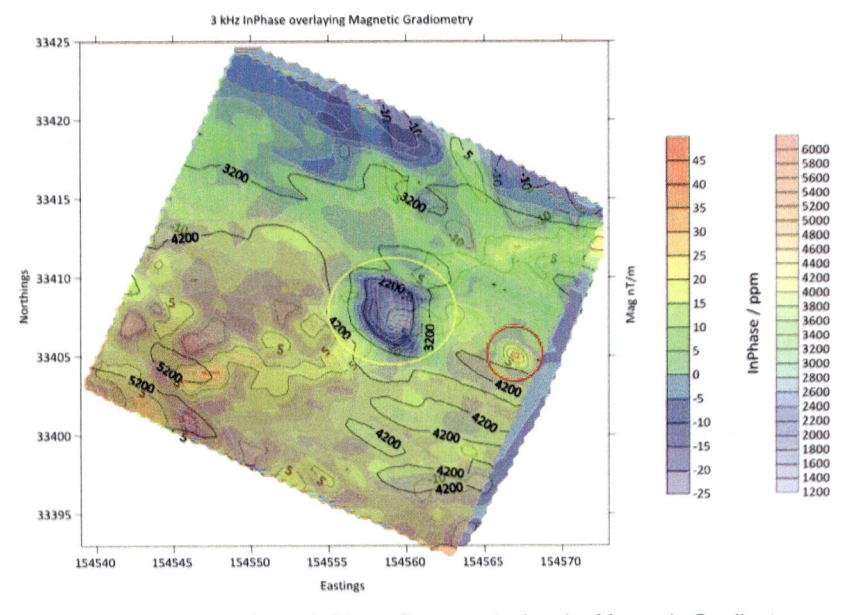

Figure 37. Showing the 3 kHz InPhase Data overlaying the Magnetic Gradient Data. The black contours (4200) showing the outline of the InPhase.

When these data sets are overlaid their images clearly show a relationship between the different geophysical methodologies. The ability of the InPhase to act as a heavy-duty metal Detector potentially showing the outline of the clean or metal free back fill following the CAU investigation (yellow oval). The red circle denotes the MAG anomaly in figure 24.

39

Fig 25.

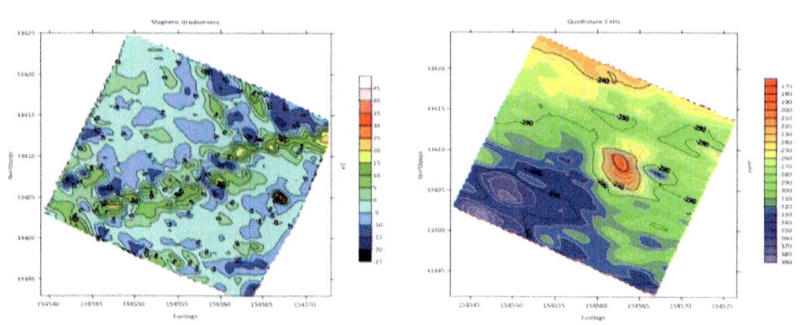

660058953. CSM M118 Surveying, Land and Environmental Management.

Figure 24. Data from above (different colour pallet)

Figure 32. 3 kHz Data from Above (in a

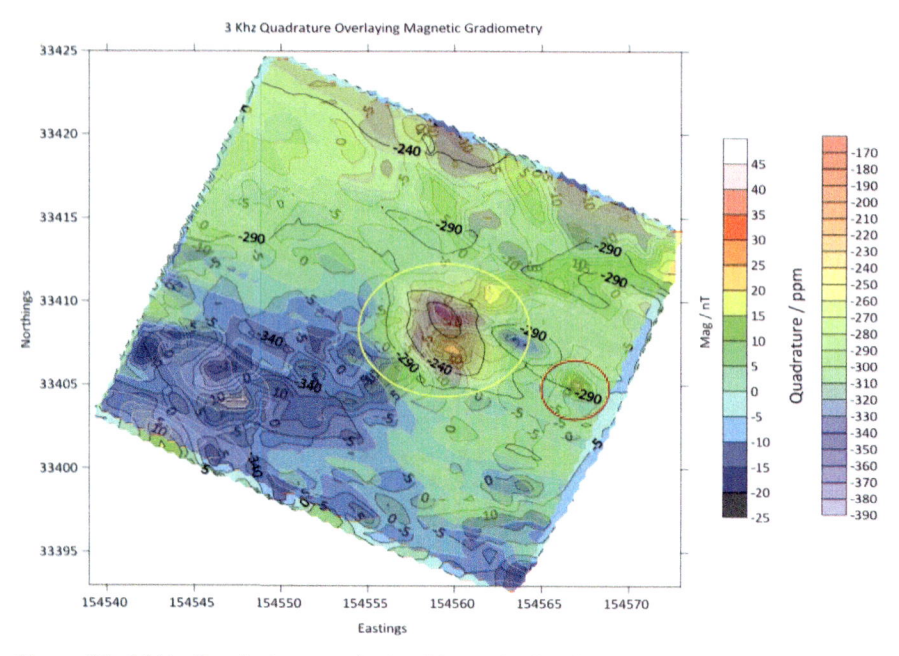

Figure 38. 3 kHz Quadrature overlaying Magnetic Gradiometry Data

As above the overlay of the 3 kHz Quadrature which is noted as being particularly versatile for the investigation of back fill surveys suggests a close fit with the data of the Magnetic Gradiometry (yellow oval in figure 38).

Fig 26.

660058953.   CSM M118 Surveying, Land and Environmental Management.

5 Errors in Geophysical Methodologies

When carrying out any form of investigative study, errors can occur in both the physical operations as well as the processing and interpretation of the data. The importance of magnetic cleanliness is paramount, followed by good planning, field procedure, recording and possible considerations of numerous other anthropogenic or natural influences. When carrying out Geophysical methods, data is collected in a raw form before being processed through the relevant software. These software manipulations can induce numerous errors or misinterpretation. This misinterpretation can be a product of the analysis of data throughout many stages and is often influenced by the experience of the surveyor. There is often more than one point of view or explanation to the outcome of the findings.

Figure 39. Ariel image showing the proximity of the two vehicles to the survey location and grid as highlighted (red circle) and the approximate survey grid in blue and white lines (24x26m) (see figure 40 below).

As with many modern scientific methodologies and techniques, each has it's advantages as well as disadvantages. Above outlines some of the more obvious errors that can be encountered but does not investigate the technical issues that each methodology can encounter. Both Mag and EM can be greatly influenced by the operators lack knowledge and experience as well as the unknown natural and anthropogenic effects created by hidden structures or phenomenon. In depth discussion of these pros and cons has been reserved for future studies. As technology and knowledge advances are made in the science of geophysics the methods and data interpretation will become ever more reliable as well as transferable to other areas of surveying geomatics.

660058953.   CSM M118 Surveying, Land and Environmental Management.

may suggest the removal or displacement of any objects or materials which might have influenced the magnetic survey (figures 37 and 38 above). The backfill from the CAU investigation will potentially have been cleared of any artefacts or material from the incident and could therefore be considered archaeologically sterile.

The use of the EM method in this application as a heavy-duty metal detector did not appear to indicate any particular targets of interest over the previously investigated site which is somewhat to be expected. There is however some indication of a possible anomaly as shown in figures 34-36 to the western or mid left section of the grid. Bearing in mind that, the lower the frequency the greater the depth examination there is a suggestion that there may be an area of future interest in subsequent investigations. The data recorded at this point may also be as a result of the underlying geology as a similar pattern can be seen in both the quadrature as well as conductivity and would therefore require further study. The conductivity results are very low (ms/m) as are the quadrature (ppm) with the InPhase data results being very high (ppm) compared to the resulting data recovered over the CAU excavation of 2017.

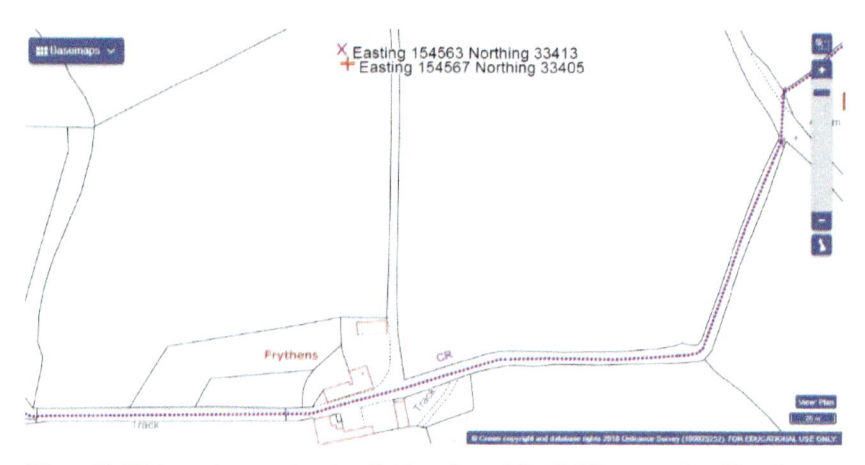

Fifure 41. Digimap image showing the location of the CAU excavation (Purple cross) and the strong Magnetic anomaly (Red Blob) sown in the Magnetic Gradiometry data (Edina 8th July 2018).

When both the MAG and EM are overlaid and considered simultaneously with the resulting data from the previous excavation disturbances, coupled with the information gathered with regard the metal detection, the data may suggest the anomalies shown in figure 24 are at a reasonable depth. They would also suggest they may well be of a metallic or magnetic influence.

43

Fig 28.

Fig 29.

LIST OF PICTURES

Front Cover. Painting by Roger Murray AGAvA (n.d.)
Fig 1. CAC Wirraway (Harrison, 1940)
Fig 2. Aerial photograph of Portreath Airfield in 1946 looking south (IWM, 2014)
Fig 3. Supermarine Spitfire Mk VC (IWM, no date)
Fig 4. Merlin Engine (Museums Victoria, 1942)
Fig 5. St Erth and location of Trevessa and Frythens Farms (Google Earth, 2021a)
Fig 6. Barn at Frythens Farm (front view) where the bodies were stored. The barn was recently renovated, but still has the original stonework and stairs (Palmer, 2020)
Fig 7. Barn at Frythens Farm (side view) where the bodies were stored. The barn was recently renovated, but still has the original stonework and stairs (Palmer, 2020)
Fig 8. Higher southerly and lower northerly sites (Google Earth, 2021b)
Fig 9. Handley Page Hampden (Wikipedia, 2017a)
Fig 10. Avro Lancaster (Wikipedia, 2017b)
Fig 11. AT118 (Tapatalk, 2011)
Fig 12. AT118's believed resting place (Google Earth, 2021c)
Fig 13. Model Spitfire made by Mr Murley (Palmer, 2019a)
Fig 14. Barry Pellow's newspaper cutting (Palmer, 2019b)
Fig 15. Pipe (Palmer, 2017)
Fig 16. Crash stage 1 (Sharpe, 2017)
Fig 17. Crash stage 2 (Sharpe, 2017)
Fig 18. Crash stage 3 (Sharpe, 2017)
Fig 19. Crash stage 4 (Sharpe, 2017)
Fig 20. Projected flight path of AB462 and AB496 (Google Earth, 2021a)
Fig 21. Julian Allin completing the geophysics survey (Palmer, 2018)
Fig 22. Julian Allin completing the geophysics survey (Palmer, 2018)
Fig 23. Julian Allin's dissertation page 34 (Allin, 2018)
Fig 24. Julian Allin's dissertation page 39 (Allin, 2018)
Fig 25. Julian Allin's dissertation page 40 (Allin, 2018)
Fig 26. Julian Allin's dissertation page 41 (Allin, 2018)
Fig 27. Julian Allin's dissertation page 43 (Allin, 2018)
Fig 28. St Illogan Church (Palmer, 2019c)
Fig 29. Sgt Norman's headstone (Palmer, 2019d)

REFERENCES

Allin, S. J. (2018) **Acceptable investigation of a sensitive protected site utilising modern geophysical research methods**. Dissertation towards the degree of Master of Science by advanced study in Surveying, Land and Environmental Management, University of Exeter.

Google Earth (2021a) **St Erth and farms, AB462/AB496 projected flight path (50°09'20"N 5°25'59"W)** [online] Available at: https://earth.google.com/web/@50.15624987,-5.43314952,10.00033698a,3335.02736777d,35y,0.00000001h,1.01154652t,-0r (Accessed: 23/09/2021)

Google Earth (2021b) **Trevessa Farm and Frythens Farm (50°09'03"N 5°26'06"W)** [online] Available at: https://earth.google.com/web/@50.15106007,-5.43505709,37.69593388a,1423.90802899d,35y,0h,0t,0r (Accessed: 23/09/2021)

Google Earth (2021c) **Rosevidney Farm and Tregethas Farm (50°09'08"N 5°27'06"W)** [online] Available at: https://earth.google.com/web/@50.15234276,-5.45170233,37.44066778a,1822.30259261d,35y,0h,0t,0r (Accessed: 23/09/2021)

Halley, J. J. (1985) **Royal Air Force Aircraft: AA100 to AZ999**. Kent: Air Britain (Historians) Ltd.

Harrison, J. T. (1940) **CAC Wirraway** [online image] Available at: https://en.wikipedia.org/wiki/CAC_Wirraway (Accessed: 24/08/2021)

IWM (no date) **Aircraft of the Royal Air Force, 1939-1945: Supermarine Spitfire** [online image] Available at: https://www.iwm.org.uk/collections/item/object/205126925 (Accessed: 25/11/2021)

IWM (2014) **Portreath Airfield** [online image] Available at: www.americanairmuseum.com/media/6320 (Accessed: 24/08/2021)

Knight, R. (2007-2021) **RAF Davidstow Moor – Aviation Crashes and Related Incidents 1942** [online] Available at: http://www.rafdavidstowmoor.com/clog42.html (Accessed: 12/02/2016)

Murray, R. (no date) **Brightening Up**, Painting, Hansen Fine Art. Available at: https://hansenfineart.co.uk/products/brightening-up?_pos=1&_sid=b7aca1669&_ss=r (Licenced for use: 24/06/2020)

Museums Victoria (1942) **Aero Engine – Rolls-Royce Ltd, Merlin 46, V-12 Inline, Supermarine Spitfire Vc, Derby, England, 1942** [online image] Available at: https://collections.museumsvictoria.com.au/items/408166 (Accessed: 4/10/2021)

National Archives of Australia (2020) **Record Search - NORMAN William David - (Sergeant); Service Number - 404315; File type - Casualty - Repatriation; Aircraft - Spitfire AB 496; Place - Cornwall, England; Date - 24 March 1942**, pp. 21 [online] Available at: https://recordsearch.naa.gov.au/SearchNRetrieve/NAAMedia/ShowImage.aspx?B=1059335&T=PDF (Accessed: 4/10/2019)

Palmer, L. (2018) **Geophysics survey of the site** [photograph]

Palmer, S. (2017) **Pipe embedded in ground of crash site** [photograph]

Palmer, S. (2019a) **Model Spitfire** [photograph]

Palmer, S. (2019b) **Newspaper cutting** [photograph]

Palmer, S. (2019c) **Church** [photograph]

Palmer, S. (2019d) **Sgt Norman's headstone** [photograph]

Palmer, S. (2020) **Frythens Farm Barn** [photograph]

Sharpe, A. (2017) **Frythens Farm, St. Erth, Cornwall: Archaeological Investigation of a WW2 Spitfire crash site** [online] Available at: https://archaeologydataservice.ac.uk/archiveDS/archiveDownload?t=arch-1062-1/dissemination/pdf/cornwall2-292297_1.pdf (Accessed: 8/06/2018)

Smith, G. (2000) **Devon and Cornwall Airfields in the Second World War**. Newbury: Countryside Books.

Storr, A. (2006) **RAAF Fatalities in Second World War Among RAAF Personnel Serving On Attachment in Royal Air Force Squadrons And Support Units** pp. 170 [online] Available at: https://visionpdf.com/raaf-personnel-serving-on-attachment-in-royal-air-force77cb53b0d0db3aa2e23613ca249a284742934.html (Accessed: 14/08/2020)

Supt. Rowland (1942) **Police War Diaries**, Accessed at Cornwall Records Office.

Tapatalk (2011) **Hampden AT118 C-VN – Squadron Forum** [online] Available at: https://www.tapatalk.com/groups/squadronforum/viewtopic.php?p=421#p421 (Accessed: 21/09/2017)

The National Archives (1942) **Squadron Number: 66 Summary of Events** [online] Available at: https://discovery.nationalarchives.gov.uk/details/r/D8452977 (Accessed: 20/08/2019)

Van den Berg, B. (2018) **Inquest of Sqn Ldr Daniel Cremin**. HM Coroner for Cornwall and the Isles of Scilly.

Wikipedia (2017a) **Handley Page Hampden** [online] Available at: https://en.wikipedia.org/wiki/Handley_Page_Hampden#/media/File:Handley_Page_Hampden.svg (Accessed: 7/09/2017)

Wikipedia (2017b) **Avro Lancaster** [online] Available at: https://en.wikipedia.org/wiki/Avro_Lancaster#/media/File:Avro_Lancaster.png (Accessed: 7/09/2017)

Wood, N. (2019) **Email to Stuart Palmer** 22nd January 2019.

World Naval Ships (2001a) **Spitfire AB496** [online] Available at: www.worldnavalships.com/directory/airframeprofile.php?FrameID=3555 (Accessed: 5/09/2017)

World Naval Ships (2001b) **Spitfire AB462** [online] Available at: https://www.worldnavalships.com/directory/airframeprofile.php?FrameID=3538 (Accessed: 5/09/2017)

Young, A. (2018) **Email to Stuart Palmer** 19th April 2018.